D0341227

Library of Congress Cataloging-in-Publication Data Available

2 4 6 8 10 9 7 5 3 1

Published by Sterling Publishing Co., Inc.
387 Park Avenue South, New York, NY 10016
Text copyright © 2006 by Harriet Ziefert
Illustrations copyright © 2006 by Jennifer Rapp
Distributed in Canada by Sterling Publishing
c/o Canadian Manda Group, 165 Dufferin Street,
Toronto, Ontario, Canada M6K 3H6
Distributed in Great Britain by GMC Distribution Services,
Castle Place, 166 High Street, Lewes, East Sussex, England BN7 1XU
Distributed in Australia by Capricorn Link (Australia) Pty. Ltd.
P.O. Box 704, Windsor, NSW 2756, Australia

Printed in China
All rights reserved

Sterling ISBN-13: 978-1-4027-2670-5
ISBN-10: 1-4027-2670-8

For information about custom editions, special sales, premium and
corporate purchases, please contact Sterling Special Sales
Department at 800-805-5489 or specialsales@sterlingpub.com.

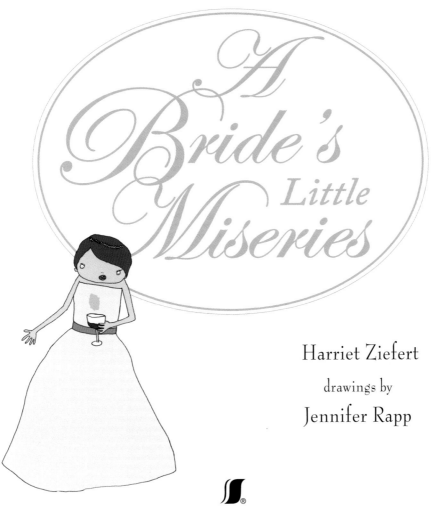

A Bride's Little Miseries

Harriet Ziefert

drawings by

Jennifer Rapp

Sterling Publishing Co., Inc.

New York

Planning
the
Wedding

Misery is everyone telling you
how it should be done.

Misery is a fiancé
with no opinions.

Misery is a future mother-in-law
with lots of opinions.

Misery is finding out
your favorite flower will
be out of season.

Misery is sticking to
your wedding diet.

Misery is selecting bridesmaids
from a large circle of friends.

Misery is a bridesmaid's dress
in the right color and at the right price,
which looks great on everyone but your sister.

Misery is explaining to Grandma
why she cannot invite ten
of her closest friends.

Misery is trying on wedding dresses
and more wedding dresses . . .
and more wedding dresses . . .

Misery is choosing a headpiece
when you don't know what
your hairstyle will be.

Misery is finding
"comfortable-ish" shoes
for the big event.

Misery is "discussing"
the guest list.

Misery is deciding on
a honeymoon destination.
Golf in Scotland?
Snorkeling in Hawaii?

Misery is working a full-time job
and trying to plan the wedding.

Misery is discovering an error
on the wedding invitations and having
to order a reprint at *your* expense.

Misery is finally agreeing
on a china pattern, only to learn
it has been discontinued.

Misery is making phone calls
to people who don't RSVP.

Misery is arranging tables
for your reception, then rearranging,
and then arranging again . . . only to go
back to the original arrangement.

Misery is making
your own wedding favors—
all 200 of them.

Misery is when your
friends and relatives ignore
your bridal registry.

Misery is writing
yet another check.

Misery is waking up
to rain clouds on the horizon.

Misery is a pimple
that arrives bright and early.

Misery is a hairdresser with a mind
of her own and a heavy-handed,
makeup artist.

Misery is a maid of honor
who is late.

Misery is an adorable flower girl
who refuses to walk down the aisle.

Misery is the clueless guest,
who steps on your wedding train.

Misery is the wedding ring that
won't slide on easily.

Misery is a bossy photographer.

Misery is a DJ who ignores your "playlist" and acts as if he's hosting the Oscars.

Misery is an endless toast
from the best man.

Misery is a dizzy aunt
showing her moves
on the dance floor.

Misery is a rude uncle
flirting with your friends.

Misery is trying to remember
everyone's name.

Misery is being
pulled in several directions.

Misery is a stain

in a conspicuous spot.

Misery is needing help
in the ladies' room.

Misery is the toast
that reveals a bit too much
about the bachelor party.

Misery is the family feud
that flares up at your reception.

Misery is a cranky baby—
even though your invitation specifically said:
babysitting services provided.

Heaven is marrying
the one you love,
and then . . .

if you're lucky, you're on your way
to the perfect honeymoon
and a week free of miseries.